Mending a Broken Heart

Curley A. West

Mending a Broken Heart
ISBN: Softcover 978-1-951472-61-0
Copyright © 2020 by

All rights reserved. No part of this book may be reproduced or transmitted in any form or by any means, electronic or mechanical, including photocopying, recording, or by any information storage and retrieval system, without permission in writing from the publisher.

www.parsonsporch.com

Photo Credit: Author's photo by Ashford Photography & Films, Laurel, Mississippi

This book is a work of fiction. All characters, incidents and dialogue are from the author's imagination or used in a fictitious manner. Any resemblance to actual persons, living or dead, or actual events is purely coincidental. No part of this book may be reproduced in any manner, stored in a retrieval system, or transmitted by any means without the author's written permission.

Mending a Broken Heart

Contents

Acknowledgements: 7

Things do not always go as planned 9

Dealing with the past 17

Shannah's mistake continues 23

Ezekiel's remorse 33

Desmond's side of the story 45

What will Shannah do now? 52

Shannah's Final Chapter 57

Author's Biography 66

Acknowledgements

I thank God for all of his blessings and favor on my life. At first, I only wanted to write one book but He blessed me to write two. I am reminded of Ephesians 3:20, "Now unto him that is able to do exceedingly abundantly above all that we ask or think, according to the power that worketh in us". To God be the glory for all the things he has done for me, even when I did not deserve his goodness, he loved me and had mercy on me.

Next, I want to thank my husband, Dewayne for all of the support and unconditional love we have shared and I am looking forward to forever with you. You have read my stories and encouraged me to keep pushing to make my dreams a reality. You are my best friend and you are a great provider for our family and I love you now and always. You will always be my number one fan. I am thankful for my children. I love you all more than you will ever know and you all are the reason I write. I hope one day that you will see that if you keep God first, put in the hard work, your dreams can become a reality. I would like to thank my mother, godmother, family, and friends for all of your support and love through the years. I pray that this book and the previous book will be a blessing to all who read them. I have always had a passion for writing. I am glad to have achieved one of my dreams of becoming an author. Stories have a way of reaching people, whether you just like a good story or whether you can relate to the characters. So many of you have shared with me how much you enjoyed the first story. Others shared they went through similar things as the characters in the story and could not wait for the sequel. Again, I am thankful to each of you.

Things do not always go as planned

It was a hot and rainy day in the month of June. Shannah sat and looked out of the church's rectangular shaped window as the rain was pouring down fast and loud. The clouds were grey and stood still as a hint of the sun shined between them. It was always strange to her, how the sun could shine and it could rain at the same time. The rain reminded her of all the tears she had shed in her life. She began to think about all of the painful things that had happened to her over the years. Shannah was tired of hurting. Lately, it seemed as if pain was a daily occurrence in her life. She often wondered why she had to endure so much heartache. She began to wonder if anything good would ever happen to her. It seemed as if things would be great one minute and then go to horrible the next minute. She had accepted her role in some of the pain but did not understand why other people seemed to inflict pain on her. She knew bad things happened everyday but was tired of dealing with the hurt. She sat along with guests and family members at the funeral. There were many people taking turns giving their condolences to the family. The funeral was also being shown on the big screen behind the choir and being sent to the church's social media pages. Guests who had arrived early were fortunate enough to find a seat. The church was filled to the capacity and the overflow room was packed as well. There was also a crowd of mourners standing outside. There were large numbers in the crowd but Shannah felt like she was the only one in attendance at the funeral. Hundreds of people came to pay their respects, be nosey, and others just wanted to see or record what happened to go back and share the details with people who were not there. It is funny if you think about it but these are things that usually take place at all funerals. Shannah's mind was all over the place. She did not know how to feel at this moment. Have you ever had that feeling? Shannah begins to look upon all of the faces of the people who were all dressed in black. Why was black the color of choice for funerals? Shannah had asked herself this question when attending other funerals. Some people cried and others sat with blank expressions on their faces. The hurt Shannah carried in her heart was overwhelming. The palms of her hands were sweaty and she trembled. She was shaking so hard until she did not know how she was able to walk in the church. Shannah actually felt like running as fast as she could out of the church. If only she had worn tennis shoes instead of heels, she would attempt to run away. She thought about the very first time that she saw Ezekiel. She was in church just like she was on today. It was like she went back to where it all started. Shannah will never forget how he proposed to her that day during the church announcements and how happy she was to accept his proposal. She did not feel she was worthy of Ezekiel. Out of all the women he could have had, he chose her. He made her feel loved and special. She had always heard of a soul mate but she never believed in them until she met Ezekiel. As long as Shannah had Ezekiel, she felt they could conquer anything. So many couples focus on the wedding and not the marriage. The wedding did not matter to Shannah, which is why she let Miranda handle everything with the planning. Shannah was just happy to be Ezekiel's wife and finally someone's one and only love. Life was so simple then and now her life was in total chaos and more complicated than she ever had known. She felt her eyes becoming watery again. Tears begin to form in her eyes and then pour down her face. At that moment, she realized just how much she missed Ezekiel. She thought about those piercing eyes of his and how he once had made her feel so lucky to be his wife. She could just look in his eyes and feel that everything would be alright. Shannah had always loved the engagement ring with the one red ruby surrounded with diamonds. Ezekiel wanted her to have a ring that was as unique as she was. She stopped wearing the engagement ring and wedding band when they divorced. Death has a way of making you look back over your life. She sat and twirled the engagement ring around her right ring finger. She wore it on the opposite hand once their marriage was over. She was glad she had kept it now. She had flushed the wedding band down the toilet after the incident with Keisha. She still regrets that decision to this day. Heartache will make you do some strange things. She thought about her twins Anna and Janna and how much they had grown up. She had not been a good mother to them lately. She loved them but had gotten so wrapped up in everything going on in her life until she never spent any quality time with them anymore. Shannah felt selfish and ashamed. Her choices not only affected her but they hurt her children. She was given an opportunity to be a mother and she took it for granted. She missed so many moments that could have been sweet memories. Shannah thought about her parents and how she had basically ignored them but they did not ignore her. Every opportunity they had; they would try to reach out to her but Shannah did not need a reminder of what she was doing wrong. She knew in her heart she was wrong and cut off all contact with anyone that reminded her. That was the main reason she stopped going to church. She did not want to hear any sermons or see any of her family. She certainly did not miss the stares of the judgmental people that thought they knew your business and judged you. Some played like their life was perfect but never told of their mistakes or their family mistakes.

There were also some that gave an encouraging word and did not give you the evil eye. They had love and showed compassion. Shannah told herself these excuses to justify her not attending church anymore. She had also stopped all communication with her best friend. Miranda was constantly reaching out to her but her mind was only focused on Desmond. For some reason she could not let him go. So much had happened leading up to the funeral. She felt as though she had no one but herself now. She closed the door to everyone that was close to her. Shannah had so many regrets. She had made so many bad choices and felt that she was now reaping the consequences. Shannah knew God was not pleased with her life and now she was not happy either. She had repented once again and vowed to make a clean start from this day forward. Shannah wondered could she heal from the damage of having a broken heart. She had caused her own heart so much damage and allowed other people to do the same. Today is the day she realized she wanted to do damage control to her broken heart, so she could begin the healing process. She wanted to put all of this behind her and move on with her life. The pastor had finished the eulogy but Shannah never heard a word that was said because her mind was in a million places. She was glad the funeral was almost over. The funeral home director and staff were opening the casket for one final viewing. Shannah debated on whether she should go or not. She probably should not have attended the funeral. Shannah always begin to question herself whenever she was nervous. Before she could talk herself out of going, the usher was standing at her pew motioning for her to walk to the end of the aisle. She had worn a navy-blue suit, with a beige colored blouse and a navy-blue hat. The wide hat was pulled down over her shoulder length reddish brown hair and stopped just over the top of her eyes. She wore a pair of dark shades to hide her red and puffy eyes. There was mascara and make up on the handkerchief she used to wipe her tears. She probably looked a mess at this moment. Shannah also hoped no one recognized her. She thought back to a sermon she once heard, "you can hide from man but not God". She had on 4 inch blue and white pumps and a pearl earring and necklace set. She stood up and took some deep breaths. Shannah begin to walk to the end of the pew and stepped into the aisle. She walked slowly down the long aisle to the front of the church and suddenly felt cold as ice. She began sweating profusely and her heart began to race really fast. Shannah then passed out just before making it to the coffin.

Dealing with the past

My name is Shannah and I am sure you remember all of the drama that happened during and after my divorce from Ezekiel. I know you did not forget about Desmond. You probably thought that I had gotten my life back on track and Ezekiel and I had remarried. We were raising our girls together and all was forgotten and forgiven. If you thought that, you were sadly mistaken. I actually thought about Desmond more after his arrest. When our eyes met that day in the library, I just stared at him. I thought back to the first time we met. I hate to admit it but I ended up falling in love with a monster. There were warning signs that came along with Desmond but I chose to ignore all of the warnings. His short dreadlocks framed his face and it seemed to be a small portion of remorse in his eyes. He has deceived me so many times until I do not trust my own judgment at this time. That look of remorse may be more of a look of guilt for getting caught in one of his many schemes. I do not understand why he would continue to lie to so many people. As the police escorted him out of the conference room, in handcuffs, I laughed. I knew it was wrong to laugh at someone when they were down but it felt good that he was finally getting what he deserved. I thought back to when Lucinda called me (you remember her; the wife he said did not exist). I remember how she knew all about me and I did not know anything about her. I thought about how Desmond wanted revenge on Ezekiel for something that happened so many years ago in school. It all sounds childish but I guess some people cannot let go of certain things that happen in the past. There are a lot of people who dislike people for things they have done as a child. Some hurt stays with you a lifetime if you don't let it go. It is funny how we can go years holding on to grudges. We roll our eyes and refuse to speak to some people who may have hurt us in the past. The sad thing about that is sometimes, the other person is totally clueless they hurt your feelings. If we do not address those issues, they turn in to hatred and resentment and you become unaware of how it affects you and your life. We all deal with things in our childhood that have an effect on us as adults. Desmond was one of those people that had trouble with letting things go. I guess we all have issues. As I sit judging and talking about Desmond having trouble letting the past go, I feel like a hypocrite because I have the same problem. I had to pause for a minute to laugh at myself. It is easy to judge others but we need to look at our own lives. I am guilty of not letting go of the past. I wanted revenge on Ezekiel for Keisha. I could not let go of the embarrassment he caused me and immediately felt the need for revenge. I let Keisha get in my head and I blamed her for causing the distance in our marriage. I begin comparing myself to her and felt I had to change who I was. In all honesty, I was never happy with myself and that was not Keisha's fault. I should have never given her or Ezekiel that much power over my life. I understand now why the scripture says, "Vengeance is mine". I made a bigger mess of things trying to fix them myself. I should have let God fix things and none of this would have happened. I can apply this same thought to all the areas in my life. It was still hard to believe that Desmond had 14 children, a wife, and several girlfriends. I think Desmond lied so much that even he started to believe the lies. Maybe the time in jail would give him time to reflect on his life and maybe he will change. I felt sorry for him, disliked him, and loved him all at the same time. After everything that had happened, you would think Desmond would be the last person I would be thinking of. Miranda knew I had a vulnerable side and could tell if my mind was somewhere it should not be. She read my mind and quickly said, "Get your mind off that demon". She startled me and I asked her, "What are you talking about?" She then put her hand on her hip and raised her voice and said, "There is only one demon I am talking about and you know his name is Desmond". She continued to rant out loud about how she could not understand how he had complete mind control over me and he would never pull a stunt like that on her. Miranda then made a comment that made me smile. She asked me, "Why did the best friend cross the road?" I shrugged my shoulders, she then replied, "to save her best friend". She was the queen of corny jokes. She would often make me laugh. Miranda then took my hands and told me how much she loved me and it was time for me to let Desmond go. I knew she was right. She then begins to tell me how much I was loved and how much my girls needed me. She reminded me of the love my mom and dad had for me too. Miranda then reminded me it was time to put the situation with Ezekiel behind me too. She said she knew he hurt me but it was time for me to heal from the hurt. She said she could see the pain in my eyes every time I saw him, even though I never said a word. She told me how beautiful I was and she was drawn to my kind spirit. Miranda told me, "do not let bad experiences change the beautiful soul you have inside". She then hugged me and said it was time to leave the library. Even though Miranda was my best friend, she felt more like my sister. I admired her strength and it was in moments like this where I felt I had strength too, even though it was only temporary. Sometimes I think back and wonder if my life would have been different if I had the courage and strength like Miranda. I made a note to myself at that moment, to stop comparing myself to other people. One thing is for sure, I am happy she is a part of my life. She always had a way of correcting me and loving me all at the same time. We left the library that day but unknown to Miranda; I left a part of myself there too.

Shannah's mistake continues....

My parents always taught me that in life, we all make mistakes. They encouraged me when this happens (because no one is exempt), learn the lesson and do not repeat the same mistake twice. It is a simple statement and it is very true. I have also learned that sometimes I had a hearing problem when it came to listening to my parents. When I did not want to listen, I basically tuned them out. It was like their mouths were moving and I ignored what they were telling me. Henry and Sarai were heavy on my mind today. Their wisdom and the things they taught me always came to my mind when I was thinking about doing wrong things. They both were constantly reaching out to me but I was in a low place and did not want to see the look of disappointment in their eyes. My mom and dad always supported me but did not agree with the bad decisions because they knew it was going to be consequences for my actions. I understood that even though I was grown, they still wanted the best for me. I just did not want to hear it. It was just easy to cut off all communication with my parents. I knew that they would never approve of Desmond. About 6 months after Desmond was arrested, he started calling me. At first, I was shocked he would even reach out to me. There were so many questions that began to race through my mind. I wanted some sort of closure. How did he get my phone number? What harm could it cause me if I answered? Why was he calling? My life was definitely on a roller coaster. Ezekiel and I still shared custody of Anna and Janna. I was busier at work since I was in a supervisor position now. I basically met the essential needs of the girls and was too exhausted to do anything else when I got home. They begged for my attention but I just gave them their cell phones to keep them entertained and welcomed the weekends they would be with their dad. I always felt guilty when I treated my girls this way. I think back to the child I lost. I wonder what life would be like if I had 3 children instead of 2. My heart still grieves for that child every year that passes. I do not think I will ever get over it. Sometimes I wonder does Ezekiel think about the miscarriage. I just push those thoughts away when they come to my mind. Miranda and my parents had constantly reminded me about being a better mother to the girls. They would leave voice mails and even wrote me letters once I cut off communication. I was kind of tired about everyone's opinion of how I should take care of my children and what I should do with my life. Desmond was constantly calling; I even had my number changed. That stopped the calls for about a month and then he got my new phone number and the calls continued. I rejected all of his phone calls. I kept hearing a calm voice in my mind telling me to not answer the call. A scripture came to my mind reminding me about confusion and where peace comes from. I thought Desmond would stop calling and leave me alone but then he started to write me letters. He wrote letter after letter, expressing his sincere apologies for everything that had happened. He admitted to deceiving me and begged for my forgiveness. I still find it unbelievable that he would admit to lying. Every two weeks, I would receive a letter. I had kept this from Miranda. So much had happened since that day in the library. Miranda was now married to Dennis. The two of them were so happy together. He loved her so much. They had known each other almost their entire lives and had always been friends. Dennis was one of Miranda's best friends. I had always told Miranda I thought he liked her but she always brushed me off. Dennis always gave her a male perspective on things. After a series of failed relationships, they decided to date each other. They already knew each other likes and dislikes. They knew the good and the bad and they put the past behind them and found happiness with each other. They only dated for two months. I know that is such a short period of time but they did not want to wait any longer. They married on the beach in a small and private ceremony. One might say the day was perfect. It was just before sunset. The sound of the waves splashing on the beach was musical. The water was turquoise and blue and contained hints of green. There was a cool breeze blowing so softly. It felt magical. I stood by Miranda as she spoke her vows and Ezekiel stood by Dennis. They were friends just like Miranda and me. Miranda wore a simple yellow sundress that stopped just mid knee. There were crystals with diamonds and pearls on the straps. She held a bouquet of white roses with a yellow ribbon that was secured with seashells to tie in the beach theme. It was simple but really elegant. Ezekiel and Dennis had become friends over the past year. He had asked Ezekiel to stand in as his best man and he agreed. I wish I could find peace with Ezekiel again but I just pushed that thought to the back of my mind. Seeing Miranda and Dennis so happy was just a reminder of what I had once with Ezekiel. They had so much chemistry between them. As they kissed, fireworks went off over the beach. It was a surprise that Dennis had planned for Miranda. It was so beautiful. It is obvious they are in love and the love radiates to anyone in their presence. Miranda deserves happiness too. No matter how busy Miranda was, she made sure to check on me. No matter how much time lapsed, we always picked right up where we left off. I never heard anything repeated that was shared in confidence. I did not have to worry because Miranda had my best interest at heart. Even if someone asked her about something that may be going on with me, she would not tell you a thing, she would tell you to ask me for yourself. Her loyalty to me was a gift and I gave it to her in return. If you are fortunate to have such a friend, cherish them because they are rare. I felt bad keeping from her that I was talking with Desmond again. I knew she would try to talk some sense into me but I did not want to hear her opinion or my parents. She received a promotion on her job and constantly traveled and Dennis was with her every step of the way. He worked from his computer so he was able to travel with Miranda and take his work with him. Seeing how happy Miranda was, once again, made me miss the happiness I once had with Ezekiel. I begin pouring myself into my job as a distraction from life. I should have put in more times with the girls and before I knew it, my mind was back on Desmond. Ezekiel was trying so hard to rebuild the trust that was lost. Every time we saw each other, he reminded me of his love for me and that he would be waiting for me no matter how long the wait would be. He would then take the girls and leave. He never pressured me. I saw the changes and growth since our divorce. He was not the same person and had changed for the better. He practically poured all of his time into his work and our daughters. They loved their father so much. I wish I could just forget everything and love him like I once had in the past. He had proved he was a better person and learned from his mistakes. We should all learn from our mistakes and strive to become a better person. I do not know why I could not forget about Keisha. It was obvious Ezekiel had no further contact with her and every time I thought about a future with him, my mind went back to the day in the hotel room and I became angry all over again. I was letting this thing consume me and that was not good. Since I could not let go of the past, I begin to make bad choices. I found comfort in the things of the past. The funny thing about doing things that are wrong is you cannot see the consequences that will occur. You know when you are wrong. Your gut feeling starts to kick in and remind you. Either you will ignore it or change and do better. Deep down inside I was so ashamed of feeling this way, I could have easily called Miranda or my parents but I did the opposite. I hid it and did not want anyone to know how I really felt. I begin to isolate myself from everyone out of fear of others being judgmental. The world is full of judgmental people and I try to steer clear of them. Sometimes the church is full of them. If they could only see, if they could stop being judgmental, they could help more people. This was when I stopped going to church. I knew I was wrong and did not need to be reminded of it. I know deep inside that I should not have let people stopped me, because the church is for the broken. It was just another excuse I used in justifying my wrongdoing. Before I knew it, I was writing Desmond back and looking forward to receiving his letters. I made sure my cell phone was charged and I kept it on me at all times. I never knew when Desmond would be able to call me since he was in prison and I did not want to miss a call. Every month I would go and mail him packages to be sure he had what he needed. I knew Desmond may not be honest in telling me he had changed but it was a chance I was willing to take. I took it a step further and begin to visit Desmond after I was approved as one of his visitors. He still looked the same minus the dreadlocks and he still had the same effect on me as always. I felt as though I loved him and he loved me. I begin to send him money to go on his account. Every month on the tenth, I would wait in line at the wire transfer desk at the grocery store to send him money. There were so many other people in line waiting to do the same thing. The cashier always made an announcement over the intercom if you were sending money to an inmate; please get in the line to the right. This was always so embarrassing to me. It was no one's business what we were doing. A simple sign could have made the same statement. It was always the same lady in line with me every week. She looked familiar but I never asked her name. She just told me she was sending money to her boyfriend and waiting on him to be released so they could be a family again with their two children. I shared with her I was wiring money to my boyfriend and once he was released, we would be getting married. We both talked about our day as we waited in line just to pass time. I noticed her because we always came to wire money at the same time. It is good to know that I am not the only one in this position. I made sure it was money I made in overtime so it would not affect my bill money. I knew he could not physically do anything for me but I did not care. He told me he had finally gotten his divorce from Lucinda and we could finally be together once he was released. I kept this secret to myself and went on with my life waiting on the release date. I only had one more year to wait and it would be here before I knew it.

Ezekiel's remorse

My name is Ezekiel but of course you know who I am. Shannah has talked about me. I know you have heard about all of the wrong things I have done. People tend to see the bad in someone immediately and forget the good. We all have done things we are not proud of and my past fits that description. Just remember it is always three sides to a story. The first side is the truth; the next side is Shannah's side of the story and finally my side of the story. I have to agree with everything Shannah has told you about me. I know you find that hard to believe. One thing I have learned in life is to be truthful about everything. Even as a child growing up, if I did something, I would admit it, accept the consequences for my actions and keep moving. I made a disaster of things with Shannah and our marriage. I do not know what I was thinking ever getting myself involved with Keisha. I am also embarrassed to say that Keisha was not the only one. Shannah never found out about Drea. I was talking with Drea at the same time I was talking to Keisha. Nothing ever happened between us but I know Shannah would be devastated if she ever found out. It was only phone conversations and a random exchange of $20 to $50 dollars here and there to help on a bill or something Drea needed at the time. I met her at the local curb store, exchanged numbers and that was basically it. It was short lived because after the mess with Keisha, I threw my extra cell phone in the garbage can. It did not take me long to realize having multiple ladies was not for me. I should have learned this before I got married and I would not be in the mess I am now. First of all, I did not love Keisha or Drea. Shannah was the only woman I ever loved. That is the reason I married her and I will always love her. Our children are an extension of that love. I know you may ask the question, if I loved Shannah so much, how did I end up in the bed with Keisha? The answer is simple, temptation knocked on my door and I answered. I do not blame anyone but myself. I could have easily stopped things before it got too far, but I kept right on talking to Keisha. The more Shannah and I argued, the more time I spent with Keisha. She was having problems in her marriage and so was I. We knew each other from college. We never dated but were in several classes together and the same organizations. We spoke and had casual conversation. After college, I did not see Keisha anymore until she began working at my job. She was the dispatcher for the trucking company. It all was innocent at first. We spoke and only talked if it was related to work. To be honest with you, that is the way it should have stayed and we would not be where we are today. One day, I walked by the break room and saw Keisha in tears. I turned back around and asked her, "Why are you crying"? Keisha did not want to talk about what was going on with her on that day. She simply stated, "Nothing". I did not bother her anymore after she made that comment. I figured she could handle what was making her cry. The next couple of weeks Keisha seemed to be fine. I guess whatever was bothering her that day was over and she was better. That was not the case because the very next day, she was crying again. This time she was more emotional. I walked in and stretched my arms out and asked was it okay for me to give her a hug. She nodded her head and said, "Yes". I hugged her to console her (first mistake). When I hugged her, she just fell in my arms. For a moment, I forgot about Shannah. It just felt so good to have a woman in my arms that needed me. I felt like a man again. Shannah was unaware but she began treating me like I was one of our children. It did not matter if we were in the privacy of our home or in public. I hated when she treated me like a child in front of a crowd. She would scold me and speak for me when someone was talking directly to me. I never said anything and thought she would catch on to me staring at her. When I held Keisha it was like I felt I wanted to protect Keisha from whatever was hurting her. Shannah had been nagging at me constantly and sex was out of the question. That is no excuse but I am just letting you know how I felt. Keisha finally let go and when she did, we just stared each other (second mistake). She thanked me for walking in to check on her. She said she did not have anyone she could talk too and it felt good that I took a minute to be sure she was okay. She said the hug made her feel better. I then stated that I would be her friend if she ever needed anyone to talk to and gave her my number (third mistake). I figured since Shannah and I were not talking anymore at home I could at least pass the time by talking with Keisha. That was where things begin to go in the wrong direction. First it started with Keisha and me sending text messages. It all seemed harmless I started looking forward to receiving messages from her. I kept my phone on me to be sure Shannah did not have my phone when Keisha sent a message. We did not stop there. We then started talking on the way to work and on the way home from work. This is where things had gone too far because we worked together too. I had told myself I would never talk about Shannah to her and I did not want to talk about her husband but before we knew it, Keisha knew all about my marriage and I knew all about hers. Shannah and I were arguing so much at home and I knew it was wrong but it felt good to hear a gentle voice. Keisha never raised her voice to me or made me feel as if I was a child. The sound of Shannah's voice now irritated me. She was constantly complaining about me never helping out with the girls. I admit I was not helping out as I should have but I did not need to be reminded about it every time we talked. We both worked full time jobs and looking back now, I could have helped out a little more. The only reason Shannah annoyed me so was because I would rather be talking with Keisha. Once the problems begin in our marriage, the wedge between us grew bigger and bigger. I would just pick a fight with Shannah over something as simple as her having the television up too loud. I would find any excuse to storm out of the house at any time to get way to have a few moments of privacy with Keisha. It came to a point until I would talk and text Keisha constantly. Early on I would get off of the phone whenever Shannah came into the room but I did not care anymore. I had gotten so comfortable until Keisha and me texted and talked right in front of Shannah's face. At first, I was only listening to Keisha's problems and she did the same for me. We enjoyed each other so much and it only seemed right to take it to the next level. I will never forget the day Shannah came into the hotel room and caught us together. I did not know Shannah had all of the angry and rage in her. It was like she had an out of body experience. The sweet, innocent lady I had grown to love was beating Keisha like a heavy weight boxing champion and then she came for me. I had to admit, when she hit me, it felt like someone had literally hit me with a brick. I had to grab her and try to restrain her but she was getting the best of me. If the police did not arrive when they did, I do not know what would have happened. It was a wakeup call for Keisha and me both. We never spoke anymore after that incident. I should have never opened the door for all of this madness. If Keisha was so unhappy with her husband and I was so unhappy with Shannah, we should have both left our marriages. The sad thing about all of this is Keisha is still married to her husband (I thought she was so unhappy). I was still shocked when she told the police that she did not want to file charges against Shannah because she did not want to risk her husband finding out about what had happened. I guess I should not be surprised, I had it coming. The Keisha I saw so hurt and upset in the break room crying that day was gone. She just wanted to save her marriage all of a sudden and now Shannah and I are divorced. I made a vow to win Shannah's heart back and I will one day. I spend so much time now in meditation and asking God to heal what is broken in me. I have a special place I go and talk with God. There was an empty lot on some property my family owned. There were tall oak trees, rose bushes, flowers, and a walking track. There was also a play area for the twins. I often brought them to the play area when it was my time for visitation. I would watch them play and laugh. They loved it here just as much as I loved it. They were full of energy and had a special bond. Even though they were different in personalities, they watched out for one another. I saw so much of Shannah and myself in them. It was like we produced little replicas of ourselves. They were growing up so fast. I would often cry when I think about all that had happened. I tried not to cry in front of the girls, but they were wise beyond their years. They were only seven years old but knew when something was wrong or I was sad. Each one with grab my arms and say, "daddy it will be okay". I would just smile at them and say, "yes, it will be okay". Shannah and I made a promise to never bad mouth each other in front of our children. No matter what went on between us, it should not take away from the love that a mother and father has with their children. We both agreed on that. There was a pond across from the walking track. It was small in size and the water was clear around the edges but kind of dark and murky in the middle. There were several bass and brim fish in the water. In the summertime, there were plum trees loaded with plums and several blueberries and blackberries. Sometimes I would just stand there, speechless, and not say a word. Other times, I would ask God all of the questions that were puzzling me. I talked with God about my girls, Shannah, and all of the mistakes I have made in my lifetime. God never answered me but I felt His presence. When I really was having a hard time, I would feel a gentle breeze. To me it was like, God was letting me know he was there, even though I did not see Him physically. I would then have a feeling of peace. It is kind of hard to explain. Sometimes I would stay there for hours and not realize how much time had passed by. I was closer to God now than I have ever been.

I wanted to be a better man and father. This pond was my place of meditation. I hate that Shannah and I divorced. After things went down like they did, I can understand why Shannah will not consider reconciling our marriage. I still love her. I think back to the days before the girls and how much love we had for one another. I keep a glimmer of hope that one day she will really forgive me and put the past behind us and we can get back together. When I try to bring up reconciliation and the love we once shared, she immediately shuts me down. I will never give up on us. I have always been Shannah's protector. I want to protect her from Desmond. I wish she could see him for who he really is. He reminded me a lot of myself. The difference between him and I was that Desmond would target women that appeared to be vulnerable and he would deceive them. He ran the same scam on everyone. He appeared to have it all but in all actuality; Desmond did not have a dime. He was a con artist and he had a way with words and would make you think he had it all but in reality, he had nothing. He was a demon in disguise. It hurt my heart to see

Shannah with him. I feel partially responsible for her ending up with him. He was so busy doing the things I used to do while my mind was solely focused on Keisha until before I knew it, Shannah was gone. I thought Keisha was the best thing in the world when I could not have her. When I finally got her, it was not all that I thought it would be. The price I paid for having a moment with her was too high. I wish I could get a refund. None of us can go back and change the past. If I had the power to change the past, I would have a huge eraser correcting so many things. I saw Keisha and her husband at a restaurant one evening, about a year after the incident at the hotel. Our eyes met just for a moment and then she looked back at her husband. They both were dressed in brown and appeared to be celebrating a happy moment. There was soft music playing in the background. Her husband looked up as I walked by and then his eyes went back to hers and their conversation continued. All of the drama she caused and her husband did not have a clue. I am so glad that she is not my problem anymore. I begin to walk faster so I could get as far away from Keisha as I possibly could. I would have run if I would not have brought attention to myself. I learned my lesson from that mistake and I am moving forward.

Desmond's side of the story

Desmond is my name. I am well known, so no introduction is needed. First of all, everything you have heard about me is true. I always say there is one side to every story and that would be my side of the story. My version of a story is the only one you need to be concerned with. People would often say I was smart, mischievous and a very manipulative man. I am sad to say that you would be correct in that observation. I have manipulated people my entire life and it has paid off well for me. The art of manipulation is tricky but if you can master it, people will believe anything you tell them. I am a professional liar and I learned this at an early age and it worked to my advantage. I would watch a lady I was interested in from a distance. I learned her habits and her ways. I would wait for the perfect opportunity and come up with a plan on how to approach them. I would then key in on their weaknesses, gain their trust and break their heart. I was always blessed with the gift of flattery. I constantly read, studied, and became knowledgeable on so many subjects so it became easier to take advantage of people. I used women for my personal gain and if they no longer were beneficial to me, I moved on to the next one. I would play on their nurturing spirit and the ladies would eventually take care of me and all of my needs. I never wanted for money, cars, or a place to live. I had as many as 5 women at a time and a wife. I could lie so well and they would all believe anything I said. Depending on the circumstances, I would sometimes tell them about each other. You would think it would upset the female but she would immediately dislike the other female and it would then become a competition. I would have the ladies thinking that the other lady was trying to mess up our relationship. I know this sounds kind of strange to most people but I never worried about anyone else's opinions. I had not gotten to where I am in my life considering other people feelings. As you can tell, I am very selfish. If I had a child with one of these ladies, they would cling to me tighter. I almost changed my ways when I married my wife. I thought Lucinda was the one. Things were good for about 3 months and then she did the same things to me that I had did to other ladies in my past. I have to admit that I could not handle it. I am reminded of a scripture, whatsoever a man sows, he will reap or something like that. Do not laugh at me! I know you must be saying, as devilish as I am, why I am quoting a scripture? From that day forward, everything changed in my marriage. My wife and I had come up with an agreement, we did whatever we wanted and we still remained married. I did not care one way or the other so it did not matter to me. Something changed in me when I saw Shannah. She was a different type of woman. You ever meet someone and felt like they were meant for you and you only. I have always felt that way about her. I would say I almost loved her. She just did something to me. I made it my business to make her mine. Shannah reminded me a lot of Deanne. Deanne was the first girl to break my heart. I will never forget her or her sister Stephanie. We were in junior high. I would always slip notes in her locker but never put my name on them. I would fold the note in a pattern and each section contained a message. Deanne actually liked the notes because I would see her smile, as she read them. I would always be late for my next class watching her from a distance. One day I was in the process of slipping a note in her locker and Stephanie saw me. She went straight to Deanne and told her that I was the one leaving the notes. They both laughed at me and begin to make fun of me. This entire experience crushed my heart because in private Deanne was nice to me. I did not understand why she acted totally different around her sister. Stephanie then grabbed the note and began to show it to other girls in our class and got them to start making fun of me too. So for about a month I had to hear this mess go on and on until the next big thing happened in school. I made it a point then that I would hurt females before they hurt me. I know you are probably saying, "How can I let one thing affect me forever"? I would not have an answer for that question. I know we were all in junior high and young and were children and I should have let it go but I just know that Shannah reminded me of Deanne. I begin watching her and I learned her schedule and we begin talking and the rest is history. I would feed Shannah just enough lies to make her feel as if she was the most important person in my life. It worked every time. I repeated the same scheme on every female. This eventually led ladies to feel like they could trust me. Once I earned their trust, they would open up to me. Some would share their deepest secrets with me and after learning this information I would go in a little deeper. I would tell her she was special and we had the agape love that is mentioned in the scripture. After that I did not have to do anything else. The female would be so in love with me. I would play nice for a month, give them a large amount of money to use for whatever they needed and then I would give them an excuse that my job kept me busy. They fell for the lie each time because I had gained their trust. Some would even prepare my food for me to eat at my job. This all worked in my favor after Ezekiel hurt Shannah. I would give her all of my time and listened to everything she said and sometimes I would cry with her. If I knew it was going to be a day, I needed to be a little emotional, I would keep onions in a cooler in my trunk. I would chop them up and keep in zip lock bags to conceal the scent. I would then come up with some excuse to leave out and then go and sniff the onions to make sure the fumes would get in my eyes. I could then cry right along with the lady and she would think I was so emotional with her and cared for her. I know this sounds cruel but it is what it is. I would use the off time to be with other ladies and run the same scheme on each one. If I came across someone like Miranda, I kept it moving. I had found out that Miranda was her friend and they were different. It was hard to believe that they were even friends. Miranda never would have fallen for my lies so I did not waste time on ladies like her. There were too many other options. Options was the password to the separate log in on the file that I kept on my cell phone. This was a way I could keep track of everyone. I had pictures of the ladies, their family, contact information and anything I could find on them. It was like school for me. I learned all of their information so I could manipulate the ladies easier. I remember as a child, my mom told me I was just smart enough to get myself in trouble. I had gotten away with so much until I did not see a need to change. It became easier and easier. Sometimes I would also learn the one friend of theirs that I could manipulate to sweeten the deal. I learned that when she went to that friend for encouragement, that friend would persuade them to see things from my point of view. In situations like that, I would still win. Shannah was a special option. I had to let my guard down just a little to get to her heart. This can be dangerous because you had to show yourself a little vulnerable and you start to feel compassion. That is a quick way to fall in love. These are feelings I kept sealed away in my mind along with my conscience. I made a point to get Shannah isolated from the ones who cared about her so I could be in complete control. If Shannah is not smart enough to figure out who I really am, then it is her fault. She should not be so gullible.

What will Shannah do now?

How did I find myself right back with the man who lied to me, hurt me, and broke my heart? The same man who told me he was divorced but was married. How did Desmond find his way back into my heart again? He is the same man who has deceived me so many times. I do not have an answer to that question. I often wondered the same thing. The same man that has so many children he does not provide for, but yet I trust him to take care of me. I figured I would go ahead and get all of the bad things about him out in the open. For some strange reason, it seemed like I could not let go of Desmond. I had experienced so much hurt in my life, until I felt this was the new normal for me. No matter what relationship I was in, I ended up getting hurt and heart broken. I lost count of all of the heartbreaks in my life. The only relationship that did not hurt with a man in my life was the bond I had with my father. It does not make sense for me to push my dad away since he is the only man to never hurt me, but that is exactly what I did. I know daddy had to be so unhappy with me right now. I remembered growing up and he would pick me and throw me up in the air and catch me every time. This always worried my mother because she was afraid, he would drop me. I never worried about falling because I trusted daddy to catch me every time and that is what he did. He always told me I was beautiful and special. Every chance he got, he would hug me and remind me how much he loved me and no matter how old I got, I would always be his princess. I never wanted to disappoint my father, even as an adult. I think it hurt me more to disappoint him and I think that's why I pushed him away. I loved my mom too but my dad and I were close. Ezekiel even went to my dad and apologized for everything he did in destroying our marriage. I was shocked when my dad told he had come by and talked to him. Ezekiel probably was afraid my dad would come after him for hurting his daughter. Ezekiel did not know I realize I was paying attention more than he realized when things started going in the wrong direction for us. I knew he would talk to Keisha right in front of my face and I just did not know who she was at the time. He thought he was getting away but he was not. Every time it happened, a little more of the love I had for him disappeared. It had gotten to the point where I was hurting so bad until I had to find out what was causing him to be so distracted from me. That was the day I caught him with Keisha. That was the end of our marriage for me. I love hard and once you break my trust; it is pretty much over with. Somewhere in the back of my mind, I had a feeling it would end up being a disaster with Desmond but it was a chance I was willing to take. Any time I had a feeling that it would not work out, I ignored those thoughts. I especially pushed the thought of how I could give Desmond another chance and not give Ezekiel another chance. I believe that is why I kept the fact I was in a relationship with Desmond. If you have to hide something, that is a sure sign, you should not be doing whatever you are hiding. I know Miranda would try to talk me out of it. She would tell me all of the things that I stood to lose, by entering in a relationship with Desmond. I did not want to receive any advice this time. Miranda had a husband and I did not feel she could tell me anything at this point that would change my decision. I know a real friend always tells you the truth and I know Miranda was definitely my friend. I just did not want to hear her. I was risking it all for the sake of love. I had my mind made up and once my mind was made up, there was nothing no one could do or say to change my mind. I turned my back on God and that was the worst thing I could ever had done. Next, I turned my back on my family. Something kept nagging in my spirit, letting me know this was the wrong decision to make. I pushed it to the back of my mind. I kept working and saving money. I even had a calendar where I would count down the days until I saw Desmond. I did everything I could to occupy my time in hopes that time would move faster. I begin purchasing clothes and other items he told me to get for him and put them in storage. I knew he would need time to get his business in order when he was released, that is why I was saving money to make the transition a little smoother. I was finally getting something I wanted. For so long I sacrificed so much for the sake of other people and their happiness. I put the things I wanted on hold in order to please other people and I was tired.

I hope the choice to chase Desmond did not come back to haunt me.

Shannah's Final Chapter

Sometimes I sit and think about everything that has happened in my life. I believe everything happens for a reason. We all make mistakes but it is what happens after the mistake that matters the most. Will you keep repeating the same mistake? Will you accept your part in the mistake? Will you become bitter and blame everyone else? Even if the mistake was no fault of yours and was the actions of another person, will you continue to hold a grudge? Or, will you learn the lesson, try not to let the same mistake happen again and move forward. This was an eye-opening experience for me. I am thankful again that God spared me. I feel it is time you should know that Desmond died. It devastated me because I almost died right along with him. Neither one of us knew that day would be the last time we would ever be together. I questioned God, asking Him why He let me survive. I do not know why God spared my life but I was given another opportunity to get it right. I do not know what I will do at this point. I know one thing is for sure. I know that I need to take a step back and really get myself together for real this time. The next thing I know for sure is that I am messed up when it comes to love. One minute everything was fine. Desmond and I were on our way out of town when the accident happened. Desmond never saw it coming. Everything happened so fast until I could barely keep up with everything that happened on that day. I had just pulled up to the facility and he was waiting for me to arrive. He had been released and he was so excited. I got out of the car and he grabbed me and hugged me and kissed me. It felt so good to see him. He told me he wanted to drive so he could hurry up and get as far away from there as fast as he could. I got in the passenger seat and Desmond began speeding down the interstate but I did not mind. He began telling me how much he loved me, as he massaged my left finger on my left hand. He had just placed a simple wedding band on that finger. He told me he would finally be with the only woman he ever really loved. Desmond said he wanted something on my ring finger to let others know I was taken. He said I would finally be his wife and he wanted everyone to know. I never understood why he felt he had to make an impression on people. He loved all of the finer things in life and always made it known. It is not a problem to have nice things but he was almost conceited with it. Desmond said he was going to complete the emptiness in his life with me. He then asked me if I trusted him. I told him, "of course, I trust you". I never understood why he always would ask me that same question, even in the past. I was smiling as he was talking and taking in the beautiful, sunny day as we traveled down the interstate. My mind thought back to our first break up and how he had lied then. A part of me wondered was he lying to me now. I was hoping he was a changed man now. He told me his divorce was finalized and he could not be happier. I begin to wonder would his 14 children be accepting of our marriage and how would he treat Anna and Janna. They had not got the chance to meet Desmond. My mind was racing with so many thoughts. The day seemed almost perfect as we were on our way out of town to get married. All of a sudden, there was a loud noise, and I felt so much pressure being pushed against me. The sound was so loud until my ears began ringing. I remember seeing a big cloud of dust and hearing glass shattering all around me. I instantly felt the small pieces of glass cutting into my skin. The car was spinning rapidly and the air bags had deployed. All of a sudden, I had a bloody taste in my mouth and it felt as if my nose was broken from the impact of the air bag hitting my face. I remember going in and out of consciousness. I felt numbness and pain all at the same time. I wondered would I live or die. I was so scared at that moment. I begin to wonder would I see my children again. The car then came to a complete stop and I remember seeing a female running towards the car. I thought it may be someone coming to offer help after seeing the crash. Her face looked familiar to me. I had saw her somewhere before and then it came to me where I remembered her from. It was the same lady that was waiting in line with me every month when I was sending money to Desmond. I felt like such a fool right now. Her boyfriend was Desmond. She never mentioned his name. She was kicking and hitting Desmond but he was not moving.

Desmond had lied once again. I thought he had changed but it is apparent now that he had not changed. If I had the strength I would hit and kick Desmond too but I remember everything going black after that. I woke up in a hospital bed with a terrible headache. As I slowly opened my heavy eyes, it felt as if my entire body ached. I saw cuts, bruises, and scratches all over my hands and arms. I slowly moved my fingers and my toes out of fear I would not be able to move. As I begin to move the rest of my extremities, monitors begin to make loud noises and alarms were sounding off and a nurse came into my room. She began to check my pulse and monitor my blood pressure. She asked me if I remembered what had happened and why I was here. I begin asking her questions and she tried to calm me down. I wanted to know what hospital I was in and where was Desmond. The nurse then left the room to get the doctor to come and talk to me. The doctor came into my room and begins to tell me that I was in an accident. He said I was very lucky to be alive with all of the damage that was done to the car. I then asked him, how was Desmond? He asked me my

Mending a Broken Heart

relationship to Desmond. I told him he was my fiancé. The doctor had the strangest look on his face. I asked him why he was looking at me in the manner he was looking. The doctor then began to shake his head from side to side and informed me that Desmond did not survive the accident and his wife had been notified because she was the next of kin. I saw the doctor's mouth moving but I did not hear anything else he said after the word wife. He died on the scene and I walked away from the accident with a mild concussion. The local news station reported that Desmond's girlfriend was driving the car that hit us and she confessed to intentionally driving the car into us. She was angry because he had promised he would be with her and their two children once he was released from prison. She apparently went into a rage when she saw me in the car with him. So here we are again with the same story as before. I thought Desmond had changed but it turns out he was back up to his old games again. Now Desmond was gone and was not here to even answer the questions I wanted answers too. Several things have happened since the funeral. Desmond's unexpected death took a toll on me. I begin to take an inventory of my own life. I know you were probably thinking why did I go back to him after all of the lies he told? I was giving him another chance again. Sometimes the truth is facing us and we still refuse to see it. I do not know why I attended Desmond's funeral. I had no business there and to make matters worse, I was trying to hide and ended up bringing more attention to myself when I passed out. I did not know Ezekiel and Miranda were at the funeral. They said they had a feeling I would show up and even though neither of them was a fan of Desmond, they wanted to be there to keep an eye on me. Ezekiel took me straight to the doctor after I passed out because he feared I was having complications from the accident. Everything turned out to be okay with me after the doctor checked me out. I am so glad that Miranda and Ezekiel had followed me to the funeral. I understand now that sometimes closure is not always possible. If I would never have needed closure from Desmond, none of this would have happened. I should have never reached out to him when he contacted me. Eventually, he would have got the message and moved on. I pray Desmond made his peace before leaving this world and he had his business fixed after leaving behind 18 children and a wife. Yes, 18 not the original 14 that we thought when this all began. It was printed on his obituary. I was just as shocked as you are now. Desmond is behind me now and I am going to start damage control on my heart today. I am starting by working on myself. I am leaving the past behind me. I have learned to love myself and stop comparing myself to other people. We are all unique people and I know my parents, children and Miranda love me. It is time I return the love. Ezekiel and I remain good friends. He has tried to work things out to my surprise. We make great co-parents to our children. I do not know if we will ever get back together again. I am taking time to mend the pieces of my broken heart, right the wrongs in my life and move forward. We both are in counseling and working on becoming better people. Who knows what the future holds but God. Desmond's life was over but I still had a chance to get it right. God has given me another chance; I am going to make the most of this opportunity. I am reminded of a poem:

I am still here, my life did not end

This time, my broken heart must mend

My life has brought me many emotions, ups and down

Sometimes I do not have strength to smile and must frown

No matter if you feel alone, God is still there

The past is gone; dry your tears, smile, and cry no more

Your broken heart, God will restore

Today is a new day

There is so much to live for.

Author's Biography

Curley A. West is a fiction author. Her first fiction book, "Broken Vows" was published in 2019. When she is not reading or writing, she is often found trying to bring a smile and sometimes a laugh to other people. Curley has learned a smile can help brighten your day and others around you. She lives in Shubuta, Mississippi with her husband Dewayne and their three children.

You can connect with Curley on her website at: http://www.curleywestauthor.org.

www.ingramcontent.com/pod-product-compliance
Lightning Source LLC
Chambersburg PA
CBHW052122110526
44592CB00013B/1718